Homosexuality
is
God's Will

Arshad Sulahri

Pharos Books

ISBN: 978-93-91103-96-5
eISBN: 978-93-91103-98-9

©Publishers

Publisher: Pharos Books (P) Ltd.
Plot No.-55, Main Mother Dairy Road
Pandav Nagar, East Delhi-110092
Phone: 011-40395855, +14049995474
WhatsApp: +91 8368220032
E-mail: sales@pharosbooks.in
Website: www.pharosbooks.in
Edition: 2021

Homosexuality is God's Will
Author: Arshad Sulahri

Arshad Sulahri is a humanitarian journalist

Prof. Mussaddiq
Rationalist philosopher

This book is apparently a collection of essays written by a writer from time to time. But the mouthpiece of a sensitive individual and a class-conscious journalist is a comprehensive account of the history of mass movements and revolutionary consciousness in Pakistan. Until 1990, consciousness meant only class consciousness, as a politician, a journalist, even a student. Did not happen until he became acquainted with the politics of the Right and the Left. The global squabbling between the Left and the Right had defined consciousness with certain limitations. After the collapse of the Soviet Union, these constraints also began to break down and new winds began to blow. Today, in order to become a conscious citizen, along with familiarity with the Left, an understanding of new sciences and new movements, information technology, public relations and genetic engineering has become essential. Strong Right wing, allied, religious classes have poisoned new research into new sciences. While the champions of the Left see these new investigations as an addition to Marxism and call these innovations a new conspiracy of the capitalist bloc. This same thinking distinguishes Arshad Sulahri from other journalists and writers, that he is modern. He fully understands the importance of science and does not hesitate to adopt it. No one has adopted this attitude of modernity rationally and this is a clear sign of his tendency towards rationalism. We are in the world of fundamentalism, where he stands for the candle of realism. There were very few people who wrote on this school of thought and now the development of market economy has included commercialism in journalism as well. As a result, even writers with understanding and critical point of view have started writing superficial essays based on sentimentality instead of realistic essays, while a good and standard writer goes beyond emotions and makes objective analysis of situations and events.

Arshad Sulahri's writings have these four characteristics in common, which indicate his rational style of writing and set him apart from other contemporary emotional writers. His comments are human, and his emotions are in order. That is why his writings have the status of organized and dignified protest. Arshad Sulahri is considered a leftist writer due to his class tendency. But in his columns. In many places there are differences with the orthodox views of the Left. This difference is under the influence of special rationalism which is also the result of his personal thinking and affiliation with the rationalist organization Youth Farm Pakistan. Intervention is a healthy process that creates openness in experience and maturity in rationalist ideology. It provides an opportunity to see the decline and disintegration of other organizations. Apart from Arshad Sulahri Sahib Youth Farm Pakistan, the following platforms are showcasing his ideas, skills and talents and many people are benefiting from them.

- Human Rights Commission of Pakistan

- The Amnesty International

- The Disability Movement

- The South Asia Peace Movement
- The Human Rights Organization
- The Writers Youth Forum.

He is channeling the intersection of the movement points of all these organizations through his journalistic skills. Arshad Sulahri is an expert in coffin writing.

His works emphasize relevant issues. His articles are inspiring as well as informative for the new generation. They have also highlighted the many misconceptions of the Right and the left. He has kept it above the sects and has also accepted the virtues of the right wing with open heart. In particular, he has adopted a healthy critical attitude towards the PML-N and the Pakistan People's Party. In his columns, he has given prominence to the revolutionary movements and paid homage to their leaders and workers. He is a revolutionary and supports revolutionary movements but he does not welcome the revolutionary slogans put forward by social democratic parties like PPP, PML-N and PTI but call them a continuation of shameful imperialist policy and this is his wise decision. In short, it is fair to say that he has a micro-understanding of society and is well aware of the complexities of the relationship between the superficial system and the subsequent system, and its their subjects are studied chronologically, the political economy of our society. A beautiful and insightful distinction of social evolution emerges out of his writings which will be an important milestone in increasing the understanding of the new generation.

Contents

1. Homosexuality is God's will 9

2. Homosexuals are also God-made human beings 12

3. Homosexuality and our behaviors 15

4. Homosexuality is not an optional act............................ 18

5. Why is it necessary to repeal Section 377
    of the Pakistan Penal Code? 21

6. A detailed answer to the objections
    on why it is necessary to repeal Section 377 24

7. Why do women like homosexuality?................................. 29

8. Doesn't it look like something to us? 32

9. The importance of inheritance in making
    Eunuchs a part of society 36

10. Women are not the property of the market,
    my body is my basic human right 41

11. Special education-style sex education department to
    be set up to end child abuse and rape 50

Homosexuality is God's will

Professor Wajahat Masood's essay on homosexuality discusses human ethics, human behavior, human rights and the acceptance of people with different identities in society, which has traditionally been accused of denigrating and promoting homosexuality, instead of arguing and resolving the issue.

Promoting homosexuality is such that if someone talks about the rights of people with disabilities, it is said that someone is promoting disability. Homosexuality is a human issue. Homosexuality cannot be promoted from any angle. How can one attract someone to be gay? It is not an ideology, a culture or a religious identity to be preached. We need to understand homosexuality. Homosexuality is not a crime. It is not an attitude. Nor is it an optional verb. It is a matter of a person's different identities.

Eunuchs are born with different identities. Most have a dual identity. Every conscious being knows this. No married couple expects their children to be eunuchs instead of boys or girls. But they are powerless. Eunuchs are born from the human womb. Eunuchs also have rights as human beings. So, does talking about the rights of eunuchs promote dual identity?

We are not isolated from the rest of the world, they as there are people with different identities in the rest of the world. They are also in the territory of Pakistan. We cannot claim that all human beings born in Pakistan have the same identity, have the same religion have the same tendency even though everyone think the same, speak the same and walk the same. There are many other identities, including female, male and eunuch. Every human being is born with his own identity.

Man has no right to be born with identity. It is God's will and all human beings are God's creatures. It is God's work. Factory power. There is nothing that man can do about it. Religious thinkers often refer to the nation of Lot as homosexual. The sinking of the city and the destruction of Lot's people are told. Any Muslim, Christian or Jew can say that the nation of Lot was killed by a righteous and virtuous nation. Another group had drowned the people of Lot.

There is historical evidence that this did not happen. They were the victims of God's wrath. The point of all humanitarians, including Ustad Wajahat Masood, is that people of the same sex are also God's creatures and human beings. As human beings, we need to adopt a humane attitude instead of hating human beings. The rest is left to Allah. Man is not involved in it.

No state, no class, no religion has the right to decide the fate of people with different identities or deprive them of their human rights. Every human being has the full right to live in solitude. No law in the world allows intrusion into anyone's private life.

It was the responsibility of the state to inform the health department about people with dual and separate identities and to remove misconceptions among the people, but the state, like many other issues, is silent on homosexuality. Due to the lack of

Homosexuality is God's Will

awareness, many elements in the public come down to making their own decisions. As a result, countless people have been killed.

Hate people with different identities, including homosexuality, don't consider them human. Don;t give them human rights. To kill them There is interference in God's work. There is rebellion against the laws of God. Because God did not create them all. They are God's creation. God willing.

Homosexuals are also God-made human beings

Objection to the rights and support of homosexuals and the attitude of cursing and blasphemy by some people by giving religious references is very unfortunate. In the following line, I have had to resort to the words of individuals for the sake of compulsive homosexuals and for those who gossip and curse. Homosexuals are also human beings. It is human sympathy that they too should be considered human beings and their human rights should be discussed. They should be given the right to live. The main purpose of supporting homosexuals and talking about their rights is to keep them alive. No person or institution has the right to give or take their life. It is a grave sin to take the life of any human being for his unintentional act.

God loves human equality. Homosexuals are also created by Allah and are human beings. If a man or a woman has mental, physical and sexual defects, then He has not created them. Allah Almighty has created them with a special quality. It is not the fault of the man or the woman, nor do they have the power to do so.

Therefore, expressing hatred towards such persons is tantamount to interfering with the law of nature. In addition to men and women, the third sex is recognized all over the world, while other identities between men and women are also recognized.

Hate on the basis of faith, race and identity is a violation of basic human rights, which no religion allows. It is very unfortunate that in just two years in Pakistan, 80 people with different sexual identities have been deprived of their right to live. Most of them belonged to the eunuch community.

The sanctity and value of human life is more important than all beliefs, traditions and religions. It is generally said that homosexuality is a grave sin in Islam. Without research and thought, the fabric of homosexuality is linked to the nation of Lot. They had no separate identity at all. In the oldest traditions, people with distinct identities had an important place in ancient societies. They were considered worthy of love and special attention. Periods of recent monarchies also gave them special importance.

Today's era on Pakistani soil has become a practical example of oppression and barbarism. It is haram for a child, a young person, or an adult to live in the society when their identity is revealed. Schools, colleges, universities, workplaces, offices and such places should be gathered here. It is these oppressors who are teaching Islam. Instead of imposing Islamic morality on themselves, they impose it on others. This double standard and hypocrisy has become the first form of society.

The current era is one of personal freedom and human rights. The demands of today's age are to get rid of self-made chains and give every human being the right to live as he pleases. Pakistan is a constitutional state and recognizes the international charters of the United Nations. Every citizen of Pakistan is a part of the international community. Pakistan is not a country of a separate planet and is not a separate religious state that has its own separate constitution and law. It is the duty of every citizen of Pakistan to obey the constitution and law of the land. No citizen is above the law. According to the constitution and law of the country, homosexuals are equal citizens and have the right to live.

Homosexuality and
our behaviors

Connivance is not the solution of any problem. Especially an issue related to one's self which is related to sex, Merely suppressing it due to shame does not make sense. Talking about sex is not obscene. This is a serious matter. There is also an urgent need to talk about sexual issues in Pakistan.

In the society in which we live, sexual matters are deliberately mostly suppressed. Instead of talking seriously, detachment is adopted by declaring it as a grave sin and obscenity. This is inhumane behavior. We need to take off all political, social and religious masks and think as human beings.

Those whose actions we hate are human beings just like us. The only difference is that if a child is influenced by an environment or is naturally attracted to his homosexuality due to the inattention of educational and training institutions in our society and especially by the parent's side, then what is the child's fault? This can be a child's instinct. The environment that became available to her, nurtured her instincts and the elements of homosexuality continued to grow.

Parents need to keep an eye on their child's habits, and friendships because parents are well aware of their child's shortcomings. When parents or adults discover that their child (son or daughter) is different than others by their habits or attitudes, parents need to love more than ever before, instead of hitting, kicking out and expressing hatred, bring them more closer, and focus on them as much as possible. Inexplicably you can give the child a new life, a new environment. The point is that parents should adopt and not reject their gay children, never turn a blind eye from the truth. They need our attention and love, not ignorance.

Homosexuality is neither a crime nor a disease. This is inhumane nature. The pages of the earliest history also bear witness to the fact that human was both homosexual and also inclined towards the opposite sex. Homosexuality is nothing new. Nor is it created by Western countries. The only difference is that the West, like many others, has accepted the reality of homosexuality. Accept the fact that there are a significant number of homosexuals in Pakistani society. Eunuchs are different. There have also been several cases of secret gay marriages.

In other cities, including Islamabad and Rawalpindi, same-sex couples are living their married lives. Faraz (not real name) from Mirpur Azad Kashmir in Rawalpindi has been living with his homosexual for three years. Thus Farwa (not real name) and Sonia (not real name) have been together for four years. Their story has also been reported by the BBC. Social media and certain websites are successful sources for the meetings and the rights of homosexuals.

    Homosexuality is God's Will

But homosexuals are trapped in fear. The fright of parents, relatives, religion, and fear of society haunts them all the time. There is no shortage of such incidents when people killed their own people in the name of honor and religion. Three young gay men were killed in Lahore last year. Murder in the name of religion and honor is the result of deviating from the facts. Societies that turn a blind eye to reality cannot live long. We need to make our attitudes and thinking realistic. Problems arising from visual impairment, when they get out of hand, then nothing comes to hand except backlash. Ignoring homosexual children is like ruining your lap with your own hands. Life of such persons has value than humiliation.

Homosexuality is not an optional act

Homosexuality is not a sin. God created us to be homosexual, and the feelings of homosexuality are natural .Many saints have also been gay. These arguments were made by Muhammad Sufyan (pseudonym) in the response to a question about how long you have been suffering from homosexuality. Sufyan says many holy figures, including Madhoo Laal Hussain and Mahmood Ayaz, were gay.

Encouraged by the conversation with Sufyan, I searched for many homosexuals and asked them the same questions. Most of the answers were similar to Sufyan's.

Forty-five-year old Tanveer (pseudonym), a resident of the Posh area in Islamabad, has formed a large network of gays, which also holds regular meetings. With great difficulty he (Tanveer) agreed to negotiate with me, He is highly educated, married and have three children. Tanveer says it is wrong to say that bad company and friendship with older boys create an element of homosexuality. On the contrary, it is about whether he is gay or not!

Answering a question about himself, Tanveer said that, "he liked boys since childhood".'We were three same age group friends, which I would bring home. Give those gifts and other things of mine. The long wait for the day to come at night is simply because the company of your friends will be available in the morning. We still meet today," Tanveer also said.

Hafiz Noor (pseudonym), one of Tanweer's friend (who also leads imamate in Madrassa), said in a conversation that, he agrees with Tanweer. Homosexuality is not an optional act. Hafiz Noor, in the light of his personal experiences and observations, said that he was personally incapable of practicing homosexuality. "Living in a religious environment, I have tried many times to withdraw but to no avail". On the question of sin (on the behalf of religion), Hafiz Noor gave his views that sin is to harm someone. But it is a matter of love. And love is not a sin.

Tanveer also talked to some of his friends on the phone and asked them for a meeting with me. It was in Islamabad that I had the opportunity to meet Saif in the Imam Bari area. Saif's hometown is Mandi Bahauddin. The feminine element is predominant in Saif.

"Allah has made me like this," Saif said in a very interesting conversation. "I didn't want to be born that way. If God has placed homosexuality in my nature, then my action may be disliked by someone, but they are not in the category of sin. Sin is when you have the feelings to hurt someone. When you have satisfaction, there is happiness. If I am satisfied then who else is to interfere in my life?"

Saif said the biggest sin is raping a three-year-old girl. Sexually abused to young children is a crime. Saif also termed intimacy with his wife without her consent as a sin and said that if homosexuality is a sin or an unnatural thing, then many animals are homosexuals too. They should also be preached. Animals should also be stopped. "We are also human beings," Saif said "Just because we are different does not mean that do hate us. Be separated from other humans. Be considered untouchable. This is inhumane behavior. We don't need to understand, our society need to!"

Saif cried after telling his story. The fact is that, as a society we need to at least maintain a humane relationship with homosexuals. Don't deprive them of mother's love and father's affection. Cherish brother and sister relationships. After all, why don't we think as human beings? Why do we sacrifice our blood relations for the sake of religious interpretations and due to the oppression of society?

Why is it necessary to repeal Section 377 of the Pakistan Penal Code?

The statement of fear is popular in Pakistan. Fear is an effective weapon of illegitimate governments. General Zia had seized power but remained in fear till his death. The country and the nation are still suffering the consequences. Fear, oppression, and tyranny destroy the lives of nations.

The present covenant is for human rights and individual freedoms. Generations are rebelling from the shackles of nine centuries. Section 377 of the Slavery Covenant is still part of Pakistan. That is a sign of fear, oppression, human rights violations and discrimination.

The main source of Pakistan's penal code is Penalties of India. It is a comprehensive set of criminal laws. The purpose of which is to cover all the important issues of criminal law. This law was drafted in 1860. Collection of Penalties in Pakistan Section 377 or Section 377 which is a law of 158 years old British rule. Under which, certain sexual relations have been declared unnatural crimes and the punishment is ten years imprisonment. According to this law, having sex with a man, woman, or animal against the natural principles, is a crime.

The 377 law was enacted by the British Crown in an undemocratic manner in its territories which reflects human rights violations and discrimination. Section 377 has been misused since the British Raj till this day. In Pakistan, the Khawaja Sara, especially the general public, is being affected. 377 is an Islamic law and has nothing to do with any religion, including Islam, but a commission of the Crown of Britain established under the Charter Act 1833 & under the chairmanship of Thomas Babington Macaulay in 1834. The system of slavery in India was imposed on the recommendation of the Supreme Court to further strengthen the shackles of slavery. Section 377 is also being used as a weapon as a chain of slavery.

A living example of this is the former Prime Minister of Malaysia, Anwar Ibrahim. Against whom Section 377 was used politically and Anwar Ibrahim spent 9 years in jail. The victims of Article 377 in Pakistan are many young men, women, and men whose lives were ruined and some took the path of suicide for salvation. Under the guise of Section 377, the police blackmail, which is common. Especially young women are targeted for disobedience or their inability to speak. This inhumane and slavery law has been abolished in neighboring India. In 2013, the Indian Supreme Court annulled Section 377 or declared Section 377 invalid. The ruling states that Section 377 does not apply to accidental sexual intercourse between adult homosexuals (guys). There was a unanimous decision of the five judges of the Supreme Court. Among them, Justice

Homosexuality is God's Will

Indu-Malhotra wrote that history apologizes to the members of this community and their families for the suffering that was inflicted on them and being boycotted for centuries. It is too late to fix it. Members of this community were forced to live in fear of reprisals and persecution.

Freelance journalist and human rights activist Hanifa Abbasi is campaigning for reform in Section 377. Hanifa Abbasi has also launched an online petition:

Http://chng.it/bVspVQhLK2

Cruel and Unjust Section 377 needs to be abolished immediately on humanitarian grounds so that people of different sexual orientations and eunuchs living in Pakistan can escape double oppression and fear.

A detailed answer to the objections on why it is necessary to repeal Section 377

As usual, my previous article on Section 377 was criticized for wanting to promote homosexuality. However, due to lack of information about Section 377 and ignorance of the real rights, Section 377 the conclusion was misunderstood that the author was advocating sexual misconduct and rape. Therefore, it was necessary to explain in detail what Section 377 actually means. It was enacted in 1860 in more than 80 other slave states, including the Union Jack.

It is unfortunate and shameful that the shackles of slavery are such and are still being used today in the manner of British imperialism. Which literally means that freedom is only for the powerful and those in power. Section 377 is imposed to silence a person who raises his voice against a police officer and a political leader for life, including humiliating him and ruining his honor and dignity. His relatives also turn away. Under Section 377, not thousands but millions of cases have been registered in which 99% of the cases have been framed for lying and blackmail.

Homosexuality is God's Will

The 377 victims include young people, underage girls, boys, political activists, newspaper reporters, human rights activists, eunuchs. The way revenge is taken under the guise of 95C.

The following details are in line with the Penal Code of Pakistan and do not alter the implications so that it is clear that Section 377 is not for the prevention of rape or homosexuality but against basic human rights, including interference in marriage. Violation and deprivation of personal freedom is an inhumane act.

According to Section 377, a person who commits unnatural sexual intercourse with a man or a woman or an animal is liable to imprisonment for life or imprisonment for either of the two categories. The term can be a minimum of two years and a maximum of ten years and is also punishable by a fine.

Explanation:

Penetration is sufficient to form the necessary sexual intercourse described in this defense.

Purpose:

For human morality and religious requirements, it is necessary to use only those methods of sexual intimacy which are devoted to reproduction. This natural action is called intercourse. On the other hand, when a man fulfills animal desires by having sexual intercourse with a man or a woman or a human being with an animal, his action is considered against the natural requirements. The purpose is to punish such an unnatural act.

Consent:

Under this provision, the consent of the object in the offense as an excuse is ineffective and irrelevant. Both the subject and the object of consent are obligatory. The object is the accomplice. A married woman who agrees with her husband to have an unnatural act. Co-offender.

The difference between Sections 376 and 377:

There is a difference between Sections 376 and 377 with only two words. Section 376 uses words of sexual intimacy and Section 377 uses words of sexual intercourse. Also Section 377 uses words of unnatural nature. The article is further elaborated using. Every sexual act has an element of sexual intercourse but not every sexual intercourse has a natural sexual process. In both cases the effect or intercourse is maintained. Sexual intimacy. In English law, Russell and Stephen have written that in order to form a crime, it is necessary to know which part of the body the action took place in order to form a crime. Where homosexuality or homosexuality is practiced.

Penetration:

The explanation of this Section states that penetration is sufficient for the formation of sexual intercourse. That is, the presence or absence of ejaculation is irrelevant. Although the semen marks are important for the evidence of the crime. If the court was satisfied, the crime would have been committed.

According to PLD 1970 Peshawar 146, the offense is punishable under Section 377. This requires penetration, no matter how minor. Therefore, the act of this crime should be the act of inserting the penis into the anus of the object. It is necessary for the accused to prove any movement in this direction. When the accused intended to have an instinct against sexual intercourse and he made all preparations to satisfy his lust but before he could insert his penis he ejaculated, the court ruled that he did not commit any act which could be considered as an act of committing the crime of Aghlam.

According to PLD 1961 Dhaka 447 and PLD 1961 Peshawar 17, the evidence in favor of the charge under Section 377 should be effective as it is easy to make such an allegation but it is very difficult to refute it.

A person can be convicted under Section 377. Whether it was really penetrated into the anus or not legally acted upon, while one accused dropped an 11- to 12-year-old boy to the ground with his face facing him and the accused made a gap in his thighs and inserted his penis in it and stood up after ejaculation, then it was declared that the accused was guilty under Section 377. The penetration of the accused's penis between the thighs of the boy is tantamount to penetration and sexual intercourse. According to PLD 1961 Dhaka 447, if the accused ejaculates before entering, he will be guilty of an unnatural offense.

According to PLD 1959 Lahore, evidence was asked to prove that the accused had sexual intercourse with a man, woman or animal. It was natural to be against such intimacy. The accused committed such an act without any intention. It would be unsafe to convict the accused on the basis of the statement of the object while his statement was not corroborated. Except that such testimony may be considered as special weight. Semen stains form important evidence, so the report of chemical exams, examiners should be given much importance. The proceedings under Section 377 of the Code are admissible warrant, non-consent, admissible court session or magistrate first class.

　　　　　　　　　　　　　Homosexuality is God's Will

Why do women like homosexuality?

Along time ago, I wrote an article on the subject of homosexuality in which only men were mentioned in relation to homosexuality. The article was about a few meetings. The article under review is also a conversation based on the personal experiences and observations of some young and middle-aged gay women. I will try to convey the views and words of gay women to the readers without any change. This was in 2020 when I first had the opportunity to meet a young woman who was into women.

It is compulsory to resort to pseudonyms. Nasra belongs to a religious family. She is also a scholar/peeress. Nasra's partner nameed Syeda Atika (pseudonym), is a highly educated woman from the Najib-al-Tarfeen Syed family in Pakistan. In the past days, I asked her for some special talks which she had accepted. Nasra and Syeda Atika say that just as men get unnatural sexual satisfaction from men, so do women get unnatural sexual satisfaction from women.

Women who want to settle down at a house, they are not satisfied/comforted with her own man. Sexual weakness in men is also a big reason. Otherwise, if her husband has an illicit affair with another woman, she can free herself from that relationship. And when he gets married in another place, the same thing happens there, in the mind of such a woman there is intense hatred for men. That's why she seems to be attracted to homosexuality.

Homosexuals are mostly divorced women. Homosexuality for women is called lesbian in English, connected to Lisbon Island. The island is located in the Aegean Sea. A woman named Sefo is the reason for the island's fame. She also expressed his love for women in her poetry seven hundred years before Christ. Homosexuality in women in the name of Sefo is also called Sefoism. The Greeks used the term Tribune instead of Lisbon to mean rubbing against each other.

The term became popular due to the well-known practice of feminism. In modern times, such a woman is called a lesbian and this process is called lesbianism. Experts do not agree on the real causes of homosexuality in women as much as homosexuality in men, and its explanatory efforts begin with Plato's symposium. He has also traced the cause of homosexuality to male homosexuality by first being born in three forms of man, male and female, and bisexual.

A second attempt to understand this was made by the Pyramids in Greece in 450 BC. In modern times, its possible causes are explored in social, psychological, and functional factors. According to Freud, it is possible that a homosexual woman may have some of the characteristics of a man during her fetal period due to which she develops masculine traits which increase in adolescence. These are the traits that make a woman with a seemingly feminine body look masculine on the inside and she begins to feel attracted to women.

   Homosexuality is God's Will

The second meeting was with Tayyaba and Kausar. Tayyaba is an MSc student while Kausar works in a company. They both met in a private women's hostel where they are roommates. Tayyaba says that when Kausar touched her, she felt as if a boy had touched her. Kausar says she was very attracted to her and she deliberately touched it on her genitals. According to Kausar, she is physically a woman but on the inside her feelings and emotions are masculine. According to Kausar, she is also undergoing treatment.

Doesn't it look like something to us?

In Islamic teachings and Muslim society, eunuch (khawaja Sara), homosexuals/zinkhs, women have the same rights as Muslims and as human beings, but in practice this is not the case.

In Pakistan, religious pressure and social insecurity have forced ordinary people to live in the depths of humiliation. There are millions of people who are travelers on the dark paths who have to burn themselves in order to put out the fire in their stomachs, including the top-ranked eunuchs (khwaja sara) and male and female sex workers.

According to the personal research and survey of Rakim, not a single one of these people has enthusiastically surrendered to the dark paths. There is a lot of compulsion behind everyone and there are situations where the human soul trembles when it hears. For example, a young sex worker in Rawalpindi said that he does not have a father, his mother is ill and his two sisters are disabled, he works in a company but his salary does not meet his needs. For one night, he gets three hundred and sometimes 500, the client gives more if he is good.

He said that the night's earnings provide a lot of support, the mother's medication is also available, and other small needs are also met. There are similar stories of other sex workers, but eunuchs (khawaja sara) have different sorrows, they live apart from their families. Even though they are human beings, they are considered as different and society does not accept them.

Eunuchs (khawaja sara) lives in one-room homes that are outside of residential areas or settlements/populations, and even if they are in residential areas, where there is no movement of people or in a place where people do not have the pace. These rooms are mostly part of the plazas or large buildings, and these rooms are not equipped with other basic requirements including water, electricity, gas. Secondly, these rooms are usually places where garbage is dumped.

The most painful thing is that society is unaware of all their issues. On the one hand, his life, on the other hand, society does not take notice of his death, even the blood relatives of eunuchs stay away from him. They live alone and they die alone, especially in Pakistani society and the so-called contractors of religion have no rights for such people. The doors of mosques are closed to them and they are forbidden to attend religious ceremonies and festivals.

The oppression of eunuchs is also due to the fact that some of the smartest types of eunuchs exploit them to the fullest. There is a famous eunuch who also talks about their rights but exploits them more than that. There are many similar gurus who snatch the bite out of the mouths of eunuchs.

Homosexuality and homosexuals are also a reality in Pakistan, but they are forced to live in oppression and fear. I do not want to promote homosexuality in Pakistan. All I want is for homosexuals to be considered human and treated humanely. Homosexuals, like other human beings, live, breathe, and have human emotions.

Just as the genitals of eunuchs are not complete, there are some that are treatable, providing facilities for their treatment so that they can become full men or women and lead an active life. Some of these people suffer from psychological problems and turn to homosexuality, they are also treatable. So instead of hating them, they should be given new life.

But from the leading ulema who preach equality day and night to the common maulvi, it has never been seen that a person shakes hands with a hijra, sits down to eat with him, and congratulates him on the occasion of Eid. Doesn't an eunuch deserve any rights in the eyes of religion? If so, why are they ignored so cruelly? In Pakistan in particular, the eunuch is seen as an untouchable in society.

It is estimated that there are more than half a million people with sexual dysfunction in Pakistan who do not have access to housing or human rights. They have no role in society. Other relatives including sister, brother, mother, father also do not adopt them. Even though they are human, they do not have any human relationship. Therefore, they lose themselves in such darkness that the civilized world outside is unaware of their day and night and they can breathe their own way with their peers.

This is their own world in which they are brutally sexually, economically, and socially exploited. The Guru knows that he is now my slave and has no one but me. Traditionally, the Guru exploits the newcomer with open heart, hurts his ego and makes him a source of income. From begging to prostitution, heterosexuals continue to lash out at them.

Sanoli is a transgender person from Faisalabad. Sanoli was a full-fledged man a few years ago, but there was also a feminine status or feminine traits in him. At home, in the neighborhood and at school, Sanoli was ridiculed, mocked and called out with feminine names, which hurt the feelings of masculinity and Sanoli subconsciously or un-intentionally sank into a state of femininity.

Sanoli is now an eunuch or Sanoli is now the co-pair of the Khwaja Saras. Parents, siblings and relatives are completely missing, but remembered. The purpose of telling the story is to inform the situation of the eunuch (Khawaja sara) or like the eunuch and to convince their parents that these children of yours are forced to live an inhuman life only because of your carelessness and lack of interest. If a child is bisexual or is born with a sexual defect or a sexual psychiatric disorder, what is the child's fault?

This is also your blood. Appreciate them and embrace them. It is the duty of all of us to prevent them from becoming dark travelers, but the first responsibility falls on the family. Will we continue to give up our children just for fear of being stigmatized in society?

The importance of inheritance in making Eunuchs a part of society

Inequality is a big problem in Pakistan. The Eunuch (Khawaja Sara) community is more inequitable. Eunuch (Khawaja Sara) are forced to live in isolation from society. Not only this, Eunuch (Khawaja Sara) also face exploitation within the community. Due to poverty and hardship, they have no choice but to beg. They also must give a share to the guru from the earnings of begging. The biggest injustice is that the parents, siblings and relatives of the Eunuch (Khawaja Sara) turn away from them as if they have committed a crime by becoming a Eunuch (Khawaja Sara) themselves and being a Eunuch (Khawaja Sara) is a sin. Parents go through this heinous act as soon as a eunuch is born and it is kept a secret that an eunuch child has been born to them. At birth, the eunuch child is handed over to the guru.

Eunuchs (Khawaja Sara) who fortunately became young and appeared in society, also went to school. There are educated eunuchs in many cities, including Islamabad, Karachi, and Lahore, who have fought for the rights of eunuchs. At the very least, it has made their personal lives easier, but overall, nothing has changed.

Every Section of the society keeps Eunuch (Khawaja Sara) away from all their social affairs and eunuchs in every religion are not allowed to enter the places of worship. Eunuch (Khawaja Sara) are not considered human beings. It is a sign of cruelty and brutality that if a Eunuch (Khawaja Sara) dies in the neighborhood, no one in the society thinks that a person has died, but is indifferently told that measles is dead.

People usually ask how to bury a eunuch if he dies. How to read the funeral? It can be inferred from this that the living human beings are hidden from the eyes of human beings in the society. The main reason for this cruelty is that no one wants to be associated with a eunuch. The Eunuch (Khawaja Sara) must be a relative. Be a father, be it a mother, a sibling or a member of a community or tribe, no one wants to be told that they belong to a certain family or tribe.

The state and political parties and political groups should formulate a comprehensive and solid policy regarding eunuchs and make the basic human rights of Eunuch (Khawaja Sara) part of the manifesto. The following policy should be formulated by the Masawat Party of Pakistan and the policy points have also been made part of the Manifesto of the Masawat Party. All political parties need to follow suit.

All those who have different identities, including Zankha, Mkhntas, Zinana, comprehensive and solid legislation should be enacted to give them all basic human rights and the right to inherit property instead of their siblings or relatives.

To make transgender people part of the social mainstream and to include them in human relationships, it is necessary for the state to take serious action and legislate for parents to take care of and nurture Eunuch (Khawaja Sara) themselves. For 18 years, parents have the responsibility to fulfill all basic human rights, including the education and training of eunuchs.

The Eunuch (Khawaja Sara) should be given a share in the inheritance of the parents, legally entitled to inherit. Punishment and fines should be imposed by making it a serious crime to evict a eunuch at birth or when it is revealed.

Gurus of Eunuch (Khawaja Sara) should be registered in every city and buying and selling of Eunuch (Khawaja Sara) should be strictly banned. After 18 years, the Eunuch (Khawaja Sara) with the national identity card should be given and also they should give the full right to live and live according to his natural instincts and characteristics as he wishes. Guru's intentions and monopoly should be completely abolished so that Eunuch (Khawaja Sara) can live their lives as useful citizens of the state by becoming a part of society like ordinary human beings.

Why silence on cruel violence against eunuchs?

In Pakistan's society, eunuchs do not have basic human rights, but as human beings, eunuchs are not included in society at all. While eunuchs are living, breathing human beings. The state, the government, the political parties and the society are not talking about eunuchs, but they have been forced to live in isolation. There is no social interaction at all. Places of worship, mosques and churches are closed to eunuchs. Eunuchs cannot attend social gatherings.

Social attitudes are also degrading for eunuchs. On the other hand, the growing violence against eunuchs is a matter of grave concern. Eunuchs have been killed in Jhelum and Islamabad this month. She was stripped naked, beaten and her ears were grabbed and humiliated. This is not just one incident but many incidents. Civil society and human rights organizations, including the eunuch community, have been unable to raise their voices effectively. There has been no condemnation from political parties, politicians, ministers, parliamentarians.

There has also been a traditional silence on the part of state missionaries and law enforcement agencies. No one in the society took notice that eunuchs are also human beings. Eunuchs have been treated cruelly. On the other hand, eunuch organizations are also for show and for the benefit of a few eunuchs. Which NGOs use for funding, grants. The role of NGOs has been terrible. NGOs have divided eunuchs into smaller groups.

Eunuchs are no longer a community. Eunuch NGOs remain silent if a eunuch is killed. When a eunuch is tortured, they remain silent. This is disgusting behavior. The role of NGOs is not just with regard to eunuchs, but the overall attitude is the same. The situation is even worse when it comes to people with disabilities. Each person with a disability has set up their own NGO and is involved in a race of funds, donations and philanthropy by selling the problems and sufferings of people with disabilities, including family members.

The protection of the rights of the oppressed, including eunuchs, the disabled and minorities, and the provision of basic human services to them is not discussed. Only business is done. Therefore, there is a need for the eunuch community to unite and work for their rights and protection by stopping the game of NGOs. It is important to make it clear that only the state can give protection and rights to eunuchs, the constitution and the law of Pakistan.

As citizens of the state, raise your voice for your rights and protection. It is not just for eunuchs but for all the oppressed, weaker Sections of Pakistan to create a voice for the Constitution of Pakistan and the rule of law and to show unity and solidarity so that the state can give in the constitution. The citizens of the departed state should have equal rights for all, and all citizens should be able to enjoy basic human rights and facilities.

The Constitution of Pakistan guarantees every citizen every right to life. It is the duty of every citizen to suffer if his rights are denied. Make noise, demand the rule of law and the constitution. Silence is not the answer.

If eunuchs have been wronged in this way, there was a need to make noise. Why is this silence death? Has society died that we are living in the graveyard of living human beings? If the answer is no, then the question must be answered as to why there is silence and death even on these inhumane atrocities.

Women are not the property of the market, my body is my basic human right

With the echo of the Women's March 2020, my body has once again started objecting to my will and as a precaution, a man has also filed a writ petition in the court against the Women's March to stop the Women's March, which the court has approved for hearing. Last year too, several men went to the High Court to register a case against the organizers of the march. On social media, many men have been calling for a ban on women's marches and some men have been inventing new abuses for women that women are coming back on March 8.

Pakistan has also become the first country in the world in the sense that mothers, sisters, daughters, wives face fierce resistance to the mere slogan of power over their bodies and they are rewarded with filthy abuses. Such abuses are given that it is not possible to confiscate them.

The Said's man and such type of mentality of people want to have complete control over the body of the woman. The bodies of daughter, wife, sister and mother could never be thrown into the fire of revenge in enmity. Drag naked in the streets, dance naked, kidnap, rap, lose or win in gambling. Sell or buy like market goods, marry in the name of the Qur'an to consume property. Bring them to exchange work, kill them in honor, cut off their noses, shave their heads, marry an innocent girl to an old man to pay off debts. In offices, on the streets, in the street, tease, make noises, if you are alone, snatch, scratch. Take off your clothes, tear your clothes, call a taxi, call a patrol, call a Randi, a woman endures everything quietly because she is a woman and a man has a right over her body. A woman has no right over her own body to say that my body is my will.

How are these husbands? How are you father? How are you brother? How are you son? How are these men? What a masculinity? They want control over their own women's bodies. Why are they against the will of a woman on her body? What kind of religion has these ethics? Is It written in a holy book or there is a provision in the law of a country that a woman cannot have her own will on her body? In which holy book, it is said that a man's will prevail over a woman's body? and he can destroy a woman's body as he wants? whenever he wants? as he wants? can scratch? or can sell?

The limit has been reached. They are not ready to give human status to women in the society. This is an example of the horror, this brutality, and the age of ignorance when girls were buried alive. Mourning was done when a girl was born.

Slogans of the Women's March demonstrate a dead conscience and a man-less man who gives meaning to my will. Think while observing the sanctity of brother, son, father, husband, and relationships and also look at the women of your household while selling conspiracies so that some pride may awaken, and they may go towards thinking as human beings. In societies

                                   Homosexuality is God's Will

where the dignity of women is not taken care of and women are considered as a part of the sanctity of women. The destruction of such societies is a graffiti. No one in the world respects them. Humiliation and disgrace remain their destiny.

Where do we hide the cat?

When everyone becomes a preacher. Began to do politics. Began to do journalism. Began to write. Everyone is a scholar, a doctor. If you think it is your right to comment on every issue, then understand that the society is divided. The state has become a mere bundle of power and the constitution is in the hands of a few. Why does such a situation arise? When leadership is lacking, The statement of the state dies. Political parties simply take the form of factions and the goal is only power.

Instead of political parties, small groups, NGOs and individuals are tasked with making their own statements. The media has no clear direction. Newspapers, TV, radio and digital websites publish and broadcast all kinds of content in the name of freedom of expression. The main goal is to run your media and make money. Political values, society building, and intellectual development goals are missing.

Such a situation has dire consequences. The state weakens and individuals gain power. The implementation of the Constitution and law remains nominal. Political parties are numerous. Whose sole purpose is to transcend the Constitution and the law. Political ideologies become a joke. Every citizen of the country becomes a media owner and every household becomes a social worker in the name of public service. Mosques are built everywhere. Religious organizations are killed. Religion is used as a weapon in every case. The sanctity of religion and sanctity remains only to be used against others. Which gives rise to new ways of committing crimes. Morality is gone.

Everyday millions of writers and speakers are interpreting the situation created and the seriousness of the situation in accordance with the above lines and also suggest solutions. Most writers and speakers point out that everything is happening because of the distance from religion. Everyone expresses their opinion because everyone has the right to say whatever they want and whatever their heart desires they can say. That is freedom of expression.

The whole situation and the cause of economic, social and economic decline is intellectual decline. There is a decline in scientific style and systematic thinking. The development and moral values of the country, state, society and classes depend on thought.

Intellectual development builds societies and nations develop, and political parties and leadership carry out the task of intellectual development. Unfortunately, politicians and political parties have played and are playing a criminal role in this regard. Political parties and politicians have preferred power over political ideology and political thinking and have strengthened the hands of unelected and non-political forces. This ritual has gone on in such a way that politics has become dependent on non-political forces. The PTI under the leadership of Imran Khan has made up for the shortfall. There is nothing left.

The promise of decline is painful. But there are also campaigns for reform. Voices are raised against the decline. There is worry. But the need is that only an organized forum, an organized political organization, an organized political party can give the right direction to the concerns and voices of the people. Then

                    Homosexuality is God's Will

there is the need for a political party who come up with a political statement and save the people from this decline.

Parliamentary and current political parties do not have the strength to dare to come out with a statement. The lust for power and corruption of the present political parties and politicians is poisoning the lives of Imran Khan and PTI.

New leadership, new narrative and new political party are needed. This is the work of young intellectuals. Those who have political thought, political ideology and scientific thinking should lay the foundation of an organized political party with a strong and comprehensive statement and start work. Circumstances also require time. Otherwise tell us where to hide the cat.

Rasputin is alive

Aspovf apparently did the trick, but in reality, failed to kill Rasputin. The history of the universe bears witnesses to the fact that the one who was killed has attained eternal life and the one who was killed has perished. One can tell how many people know the name of the person who killed Rasputin, but everyone knows who died. Then how can anyone say that Rasputin is dead? Rasputin is alive in many forms and its blood is running in many veins.

Its characteristics, its manifestations of ugliness can be seen everywhere. The stench of it is rising from the corners of the world. From which innumerable Rasputins have been born today, and as a proof of this, they express their misdeeds and evil deeds that Rasputins exist and will continue to exist with all their shame. The Holy Father cannot be killed.

There are not a handful of Rasputins in the Holy Land whose virtues and horrors make the soul of a real Rasputin tremble and shout with filthy arrogance that even the illegitimate children have a bad character.

Rasputin is said to have mastered hypnosis and to hypnotize women and to seduce women. Did not force Rasputin's followers go to extremes. Rasputin never killed a woman, but today Rasputin's holy sons' rape and kill girls between the ages of two and five. Just look at the data of the last two years and see how many innocent girls have been killed after brutality. With what horror and barbarism, the bodies of flowers and buds have been scratched.

The beasts and savages were all apparently monks. Remember the faces of Hafiz Imran, who killed Zainab of Kasur, to the real brothers of Golra Sharif, who also sacrificed their sister's blood relationship. How many cases have come to light that the honor of daughters has been tarnished by the hands of the Holy Father?

Naive parents like Tsar and Zarina send their children to temples, mosques and churches for education, training and divine help to enhance their prestige. The devotees take him to the thresholds for the purpose and think that the raft will cross but the devils are sitting there in a trap. Apart from the sacred, the stories of lustful sons in government seem to embarrass Rasputin.

The process of resuscitation on the Holy Land is not far off. It is a story of the era. The manifestations of which have been seen with open eyes. Imagine being kissed. Which is considered a deity? Whose poems are recited? Which the head puts on the eyes? Who swears by his truth and honesty? Allah turns to Allah. Prostrate walks barefoot. You can imagine the evil eyes of this holy father are searching for athletic bodies. It is in his nature that whenever he looks, he looks bad. Hypnotism and what happens is

   Homosexuality is God's Will

that even on cold meat, young people hover, one comes, and one goes. Zulaikha whispers. And you say Rasputin is dead. Rasputin is alive.

Red Rose Day, Women's March and Leadership Crisis

February 14 is Valentine's Day. Lovers express love or renew love by giving each other red roses. As has been the custom for many years, the day of love has passed and at the same time the spirit of faith of many people has been shattered. The day of modesty also passed. Sister's Day also went. In other words, the celebration of Haya and Sister Valentine's Day is merely a proclamation. Some black-hearted people write outspoken articles in newspapers in opposition to love and hate, and many fake color newspaper editions.

He also writes a lot on social media to spread hatred in the name of good name and to show his faith and Islamic mind. Humility Day is also for women. Sister's Day is obvious from the name itself. Speaking of sister's day. The training board is made for women only. There is no shame for a man.

Men should write poetry on women's body parts. Talk about rubbing salt in my wounds - d'oh! Tease in public places. Make voices Rap Rape and kill even innocent girls. No veiled Islamic sister is required to observe Humility Day and Sister Day. Religious classes do not accuse anyone of obscenity and nudity. There is no condemnation from the pulpit and mihrab. Pride does not awaken faith. No Ansar Abbasi, Orya Maqbool and Zaid Hamid deny that it is un-Islamic and not our culture. But every word of a woman's love and affection ignites pride and faith.

The women's march is also approaching. Their spirit of faith is about to awaken again. Their Islamic minds will boil again.

Then in the spirit of faith, women were abused. Say goodbye to candles and liberal aunts. Perhaps it has been decided that the expression of hatred is the standard of true faith and belief and it is necessary to continue practicing maintaining the standard. Leadership like Khalil-ur-Rehman Qamar has also emerged, and these people are proud of it.

Last year we honored women and gave them as many rights. The media is full of news. Despite this, Pakistani women have proved themselves in all walks of life. Women's rights and equal rights have been widely defined. The possibilities are clear in every aspect. Nothing is hidden anymore. Women have also put forward the definitions and meanings of freedom, honor, obscenity and nudity, including shame and modesty, which are used to justify exploitation of women and suppression of women's voices. What is the veil of the way in which religion is used as a shield to cover the sacred veil? In this struggle, woman has made many sacrifices. Undoubtedly, women have done this in an environment of confinement and oppression.

In this created situation and political and social environment, the political parties have not fulfilled their duty, they have only been engaged in a power struggle. The political history of the country bears witnesses to this, with the exception of Quaid-e-Azam Zulfiqar Ali Bhutto Shaheed and Mohtarma Benazir Bhutto Shaheed who have done a lot for constitution making and national development. I have no hesitation in saying that whatever Pakistan has till date is due to the leadership of Bhutto Shaheed.

Objective conditions are screaming and making us believe that there is a lack of leadership in the country. In the form of PDM, the allies have no agenda for the nation. Therefore, there

                    Homosexuality is God's Will

is a need for the serious sections of the country, intellectuals, political and social activists to support the movement of workers, women marches, students and farmers so that new leadership can be born.

Due to the lack of leadership and the crisis, it is facing superstitions such as political misconduct, humiliation of women and preaching of hatred. Better leadership is a statement of progress and development. They take the country and the nation out of the whirlpool. When leadership is available, the people do not confuse each other but work to achieve the goals set by the leadership.

Special education-style sex education department to be set up to end child abuse and rape

There have been more than 5,000 cases of child sexual abuse in Pakistan last year and this year, while there are countless cases that have not been reported. In all, 15 to 20 children are raped daily in Pakistan. Ten of these children are sexually abused in their home, especially girls between the ages of ten and twelve and thirteen. Five percent of children experience sexual violence in private schools, tuition homes, factories, workshops, and parks. The number of cases of abduction, rape, and sexual harassment of women for rape is also shameful.

It is very unfortunate that the Imran Khan government, contrary to the election slogans and promises, is ignoring the problems of the people. The previous Punjab government had taken the issue of child abuse seriously and had compiled a booklet in consultation with experts on raising awareness against sexual violence. The booklet was to be taught to school children so that they would be aware of the good touch, bad touch and other sexual matters and keep themselves safe. But the change government has entered the office instead of working on it further.

In the Imran Khan government, there has been a sharp rise in the number of murders after child sexual abuse. Which clearly means that in previous governments the state was playing some responsibility but now it seems that the state is hanging in the air or the rulers have nothing to do with the country and the nation and are ruling from outside. The fact is that disaster befalls the poor. Abused children are also below the poverty line.

The Imran government has not yet come up with a comprehensive strategy and program, but the names and modalities of the previous governments' programs have either been changed or discontinued. The pace of work is not at all.

The government should formulate a national policy regarding children. Raise awareness about sexual violence and abuse in schools, children's play areas, cartoons, games, movies, drawing boxes, mobile phones, toys and in public places and this work should be done with utmost seriousness so that children are protected to this inhumane behavior.

There is a scattered ideology in Pakistani society and there is a severe lack of correct ideology. Which is the responsibility of the state. The situation at the moment is that the state and the government have nothing to do with society. Society is divided into state, ruling classes, elites and many other classes. The relationship between the government and the state, especially with society, is a serious one. There is a huge gap between the government and the people. The elected representatives of the people have nothing to do with the people. On election days, people can see the faces of their representatives. Once elected, no MPA or MNA looks back. The Imran Khan government needs to pay special attention to the lower strata of society.

Sex education for adults should also be arranged in consultation with experts. It is the job of the schools to provide higher education and training for the betterment of the society so that a balanced and humane society can flourish. Closing one's eyes does not avert disaster. Cases ranging from child abuse to rape of women are being reported alarmingly daily. The most dangerous aspect is that sacred relationships are also affected by this calamity. The government should take this issue seriously and formulate a comprehensive policy without delay as the previous governments have set up the Department of Special Education. He asked the government to create a department for sex education and promote sex education to eradicate this menace from the society.

The ambiguity of identity and the imperial culture of women

When I received a call from the outskirts of Islamabad a few days ago, it was difficult to understand whether the woman was talking on the call or a man. He introduced that Sanam (pseudonym) is speaking, and he has to talk to Asma Jahangir or any elder of the Human Rights Commission. You can talk. He said that only Allah can talk to Ms. Asma Jahangir now. Khaksar does not have such spiritual power. Let me talk to a leader of the Human Rights Commission.

Sanam informed about the whole situation. Sanam, 24, appears to be a complete girl but considers herself a boy. Conversation, conversation, hair, and clothes are made like boys. The physical constitution is similar to that of boys. Except for the sexual organs, there is a man's soul inside the fetus.

According to Sanam, he met Maria (pseudonym) ten years ago. The meeting turned into a friendship and the friendship

                    Homosexuality is God's Will

deepened the relationship. According to Maria, she is attracted to the opposite sex in Sanam.

We can't look back now. She has sworn to live together. I cannot live without Sanam and Sanam cannot live without it. The family has forced her to marry someone else. She cannot accept this marriage under any circumstances.

Psychological and identity ambiguities like Maria and Sanam have led to many cases in Pakistan. Recently, Asma and Neha of Taxila, Shiza and Sobia of Manawan area of Lahore, Saima and Hadia of Mirpur area of Azad Kashmir and other cases have been identified. Instead, the drum of homosexuality and sin has been played. As a result, entire families have faced difficulties and the lives of girls have also been ruined.

There is no trace of social, religious, or human morality left. By teaching Iqbal, Qudratullah Shehab and Naseem Hijazi, societies are formed which have only fanaticism, sentimentality, and imaginary pride. Reality, facts, human ethics, and human rights are presented as obscenity, pornography, and nudity. Numerous people of Oriya Maqbool Jan and Ansar Abbasi tribes are committed to its propagation.

Women are not just heterosexuals and farmers. There are mothers, sisters, daughters, and wives. Nations that do not respect women. Destruction is their destiny. As a nation, we are doomed. No one is straight tomorrow. The ugliest act does not creep into anyone's ears. Hypocritical phrases are posted on news and social media for four days. Then new tragedies are mentioned. This is the torment and destruction. This is the fall.

Stones are yet to fall from the sky.

It is a common attitude in society that women are deceived in the name of religion, honor, and dignity. Hair is pulled on trivial things. It is considered shameless, immoral, and characterless. It is spoken and not heard. Need to talk to Sanam and Maria instead of pushing. Get counseling from experts. The ambiguity in these identities should be removed. Don't make it a matter of honor, dignity, and religion. Look at human lives. As human beings, everyone has the right to live. This push should be ended. This culture of coercion has ruined countless lives.

AIDS is a deadly bomb

Due to ignorance about HIV/AIDS in many parts of the world, many kinds of misconceptions and serious misconceptions are constantly spreading and causing fear. Pakistan is one of such countries.

Recently I came across a news item which was about the spread of AIDS in Pakistan. The news item described the alarming spread of AIDS and the increase in the number of people infected. AIDS is the deadliest and worst disaster. Such a situation has never happened to humanity before, AIDS spreads faster and faster than other deadly diseases and has lasting effects. This stops the growth process in the human body. It is a deadly bomb that spreads and spreads massively without making a sound.

There is an urgent need to provide more and more consistent information about HIV/AIDS to the general public in Pakistan. Prevent disease and so on Preaching, educating and training at the governmental and private levels is essential to raise awareness and take precautionary measures to prevent the spread of the disease. HIV stands for "Human Immunodeficiency Syndrome". This virus destroys certain types of cells in the blood. These are called CD cells. These cells are needed to maintain the normal functioning of the human body's immune system, which protects the body against diseases. It is easy to get sick. AIDS "Acquired Immunodeficiency Syndrome" is a condition in which a person's immune system is weakened by HIV. AIDS attacks a specific part of the body that is already affected by a disease or type of cancer. In the case of an AIDS attack, a person already has a disease. Even if you are not infected, hotheads can be infected. HIV is diagnosed by a medical examination, such as an anti-HIV test. It involves analyzing a blood sample for leukemia. Positive is called positive. HIV is transmitted from one person to another through unprotected sexual contact.

HIV is also transmitted through blood fluids, blood products, sperm, contaminated syringes or contaminated devices. The disease is also transmitted from mother to child. The HIV virus is not easily transmitted from one person to another. The disease is not spread by contact with the patient, such as contact with the patient, hugs, the patient's own sweat or tears. However, the virus is present to some extent in the patient's urine and faeces. But the amount is so small that so far they have transmitted the disease, No incidents have been reported. Mosquitoes and other types of insects do not spread the disease. However, we need to take precautionary measures to avoid this deadly disease.

We must avoid all habits and actions that cause the disease to spread or occur. For sex, be limited to your partner and do not be rude and do not have sex with more than one person. Infected pregnant women should receive anti-AIDS treatment to protect their babies from the virus and reduce their risk of infection. Avoid drugs and syringes. Do not use syringes used by each other. It can usually take 8 or 10 years for people living with HIV to become infected.

If the patient is in good health and has access to treatment, it can take even longer. HIV weakens the cells of the immune system that cause tuberculosis They fight against germs and often get AIDS with AIDS or AIDS after TB. People with sexually transmitted diseases have a higher risk of contracting HIV than others. For example, genital abscesses are caused by the blisters of the genitals. Provide space for HIV transmission. People who are infected with HIV also have a higher risk of contracting sexually transmitted diseases than others. Because their body's immune system is weakened, it is difficult for the body to fight off germs. Readers Ikram No cure for HIV/AIDS has been discovered so far, but the only way to prevent it is ABC, which means staying faithful to the same sex partner and using condoms. There is no cure other than this. Precautionary measures can prevent this deadly disease.

The number of AIDS patients worldwide is 42.4 million. Global experts estimate that the number of AIDS patients could rise to 48 million by next year if strict measures are not taken against AIDS. According to Dawn, Gilgit-Baltistan, including the backward tribal areas, where health facilities are inadequate and there are concerns about AIDS in remote areas and rural areas of the country. It must be communicated and the supply of information must be continued in order to prevent the silent destruction of this deadly bomb, which is wreaking havoc on humanity from within. 4 million. Global experts estimate that the number of patients could rise to 48 million by next year if strict measures are not taken against AIDS. According to Dawn,

                    Homosexuality is God's Will

Gilgit-Baltistan, including the backward tribal areas, where health facilities are inadequate and there are concerns about AIDS in remote areas and rural areas of the country.

It must be communicated, and the supply of information must be continued in order to prevent the silent destruction of this deadly bomb, which is wreaking havoc on humanity from within. 4 million. Global experts estimate that the number of patients could rise to 48 million by next year if strict measures are not taken against AIDS. According to Dawn, Gilgit-Baltistan, including the backward tribal areas, where health facilities are inadequate and there are concerns about AIDS in remote areas and rural areas of the country. It must be communicated, and the supply of information must be continued in order to prevent the silent destruction of this deadly bomb, which is wreaking havoc on humanity from within.

We have no God

I enjoy wandering the streets on hot summer nights when there is no electricity. One such night was in Saddar area of Rawalpindi. Lightly spar/blossomed. I drank a cup of tea. When I came to Bank Road, I met a 20-year-old boy. After the formal conversation, the boy had a question. "You have a place?". I replied, "Yes, there is space." I said. It was late at night. The boy described himself in a very professional way and mentioned some additional qualities that he said were not present in girls. I decided to deal with it. He had demanded five hundred rupees. Later he himself made a discount of one hundred rupees. Matters were settled on four hundred rupees. He had offers for Kissing All Body, Blowjob and much more. He gave a 100% prescription to provide complete satisfaction. Wanted to be a permanent customer. Took four hundred advances. The reasons for this were that most people pay less than the agreed amount later or Then they do not give. Humiliate upside down. They beat him up and chased him away. I handed him four hundred rupees. Now it was my turn to ask questions. My first question was where do you live? According to him, there is a small house for 7,000 rent in a colony in Saddar area. In which he is survived by his sick mother, two disabled sisters and a younger brother. The father has divorced his mother due to constant illness and got remarried. Salam (pseudonym) said that he works in a restaurant. He got a salary of six thousand. A senior employee of the restaurant used to take great care of him. He used to pay two hundred rupees and he used to think that he was a humane and compassionate person. "One day it was noon. He asked me to come to the room. I went to the room. This was the first time this had happened to me. But I already knew about this process that it happens. He gave me five hundred rupees and gave me a quick leave. When I got out of the restaurant, I could not walk properly. I was in pain. After a few hours, I was back to normal. I kept thinking all night". When he left, he faced his senior with kindness. "I liked five hundred rupees".

"I have been out of the house since that day. Sometimes you get a customer. Sometimes three or four are found. I am taking care of my mother's medicine, house rent and other expenses". Salam said that now he works as a professional sex worker. Salam said that his regular customers include great dignitaries. Salam has become a tormentor.

Society, relationships, religion, Allah, Rasool are meaningless to him. Salam says that prayers and supplications do not get anything, God also gives them, who has everything. The poor

                                    Homosexuality is God's Will

have no God. There are many such people. Those who scare me after using it. This is a great sin. Repent, etc., etc. Repent from whom. Who is mine? God ...? God is blind. God does not know why he is doing all this. Mother did nothing. Ayat Al-Kursi has been recited, Panj Surat has been recited, Durood has been recited, Mehfil Milad has been recited, many lakhs have been recited. But Allah has not heard one. Even if God was ours, He would have listened, but God is not ours. Which only frightens. In the name of which human throats are cut. What kind of God is this that his prophet Moses (peace be upon him) is stubborn to see him with just a glimpse, Prophet Moses (peace be upon him) faints and the mountains burn? What is this? God is the name of a horror. If not, with the manifestation of God, the universe would blossom, and the sick would be healed. The whole universe would become fragrant. What kind of God is this? He has no equal concern for his creatures. Sometimes it demands human sacrifice. Sometimes he demands for animals to scarify it. We just make sacrifices. We worship Him.

Babarama of Ratanpur

Ratanpur, Pakistan's most backward village near the Indian border, had a total population of 400 at the time. Ratanpur was inhabited by Sikhs before the partition of India. Most of the houses were built by Sikhs. Which were now inhabited by Muslims who had migrated from India. Muslims also brought with them the customs of Hindu society. The people of Ratanpur lived as one family, regardless of religion, color or race. They shared each other's pain. The people of Ratanpur were a beautiful example of ancient commune. This scene was visible in one form or another until 1988. Now the world has changed. Rasool Bakhsh aka Baba

Rama had four daughters. His wife had died. After marrying his daughters, Baba Rama lived alone in an older house. Lonely Baba Ram had more friends in teenage boys and stayed away from his peers. The teenage boys who did not accept the friendship were Baba Rama to Baba. Baba used to give money to his friends. Baba Rama allowed everyone, including children between the ages of ten and twelve, to play in his house, and many children came to Baba Rama's house every day to play. Baba Rama would call some children to his room and give them candies while the children would tell other children why Baba had given them candies. Rama used to teach special games. He would hold the breasts of ten- or twelve-year-old girls and give them such things to eat. This causes the breasts to enlarge quickly and menstruation to begin. Babarama also taught girls to play games with each other.

He also checked the breasts of boys and told them to eat those things. He used to check the penis of the boys. The boys were divided into groups of top and bottom. He used to use some of them himself. He used to do the same with girls and he used to remove the virginity of girls with his fingers. Baba Rama used to play an active role like an expert trainer during special games. He would correct the position and tell the one above to do so and often he would do the whole process himself. Teenagers were special victims of Baba Rama. Which Baba Rama himself used. But most of the time Baba Rama was relieved to see them playing. Parents had no idea what games their children were playing at Babarama's house. Boys and girls, including women, knew what Baba Rama's games were. The friendship of some big boys and a few men with Baba Rama was only because Baba Rama provided them a safe place. There were five or six pairs of boys between the ages of twenty and twenty-five who were

Homosexuality is God's Will

cooked together. On the advice of Baba Rama, many boys used to work for people older than their age. Six or seven boys were such that hardly any child was safe from them. If any of them fell in love with a handsome boy and the handsome boy did not agree, they would resort to Baba Rama.

Am eunuch, not a human being

If you leave Islamabad and enter Rawalpindi, you will find some people standing at bus stops or in dark places on both sides of Murree Road. Some are found walking on sidewalks. Most of them are handsome boys. Who are wearing lively colorful shirts. After boys, there are eunuchs and women. These people earn their livelihood by selling their bodies. It is easier to talk to boys while women and eunuchs face social stigma. A teenage girl wearing a burqa. She was going very slowly. Depression was evident on her face. Dare to talk to her. As she was approaching, a boy came in the middle and the girl walked with him. Then a few other women also appeared. Chandni Chowk came. At the end of the flyover is the shopping mall on the right. It is difficult to cross the road in high speed traffic. But a sick and emaciated body kept trying to cross the road. Sometimes he would stumble and sometimes his legs would double and he would fall and then recover. This human life had failed to shake the conscience of thousands of human beings as it passed through the practical picture of helplessness. The scene was being watched with indifference and stony heart when suddenly a fountain of water came out of the mouth of the emaciated and diseased body and the body came to the sidewalk in a daze. It has been said that a sick and emaciated person is a eunuch. Accompanied by the eunuch, he walked towards the nearby hotel. He opened the myth of Saadat Hassan Manto and revived it. This was Usman. He was Resham before AIDS. How long did Resham Usman keep on praying? Where did he live? Is open sky his roof?. Bridges and shop sheds and buildings under construction his shelter?. His job is to beg and eat. It is not him in Pakistan. There are millions of such people who are not considered human. The people in the hotel were watching with strange eyes. This man is sitting with a eunuch and when he hugged Resham and said goodbye, he was taking out thirty-two. I kept wondering how they are human. Which no human being is willing to accept. Religion, politics, society, no one pays attention to Resham. There are big NGOs. They get huge funds. Big hospitals, big mosques and big political parties, big leaders. But not a single snack is available for Resham. Reshma talked a lot about her family and her personal pain, what difficulties she faced in life and how people met in her youth and today in her community. People don't even ask about it. She lives under the streets of a plaza. She has AIDS. Due to unavailability of food, shelter and medicine, it is not known when she will get Mukti. According to Reshma, she prays that she will get rid of this body soon.

Plenty of sexual misconduct

Sexual misconduct is a major sin in the dictionary of religions. It is considered the worst act in Islam. Pakistan is a country where there is more sexual misconduct than the prevalence of religion. Religious seminaries, mosques, monasteries, centers of religious parties where night vigils or gatherings are held. Madrassas are hostels. On the other hand, modern and fashionable private educational institutions and many NGOs are busy in this process.

   Homosexuality is God's Will

The epidemic of sexual misconduct is thought to be in rural areas, but later research revealed that it is more prevalent in urban areas. There is a systematic prostitution and sexual misconduct in the cities. There are countless groups of young boys and girls. The number of homosexuals, transgender people, homosexuals and women has exceeded one crore. It was learned through Facebook and other websites that their number is also in crores. Women are also not far behind in this regard. Prostitution is also growing twice a day and four times a night. The number of lesbian women is also significant. According to a survey, the number of sex workers is currently close to 300,000. According to a survey and research on homosexuality, it has been revealed about people who could not even think about it and if their names are mentioned, then the fatwas of disbelief may start. Go and have big protests. The big names living in high housing societies and their children are not only passionate about homosexuality but are also working to promote sexual misconduct. It is a sign of sexual starvation that innocent children are also being targeted. Pakistanis are the world's number one viewer of nude movies and pictures on the internet. Newspapers are full of incidents of child abuse, rape of young girls, rape and rape. This is due to social inequality and religious oppression. According to experts, sexual starvation is also a cause of sexual misconduct, provocative scenes in movies and access to the Internet. Due to the lack of guidance and political instability and religious ignorance, sexual misconduct has also flourished. To avoid or get rid of such a situation, Pakistan can be declared a sex-free country and to promote sex education. People can get out of the curiosity of sex. But the religious class has also declared the use of sex as a blasphemy. Political classes are afraid of religious groups and do not talk. The rulers remain silent spectators for power. Institutions seem reluctant to perform their duties.

It is a clear indication that the government, the Opposition, the police, the journalists and other upper classes of the country are strange beasts in the form of human beings who have no human connection with the common man of this country. In the light of the situation, it is imperative that the intelligentsia step out of social media and soft beds and formulate effective and comprehensive strategies to improve the situation, eliminate political misconduct and sexual misconduct.

Homosexuality is God's Will